Silk Elegy

Silk Elegy

A NARRATIVE POEM

Sondra Gash

Dear KrausKal,

I hope you enjoy our
sharing. I appreciate
very much for your
caring. Best,

Sondra

CavanKerry ❖ Press LTD.

Library of Congress Cataloging-in-Publication Data

Gash, Sondra.
  Silk elegy / Sondra Gash.
  p. cm.
  ISBN 0-9707186-1-6
  Title.

PS3607.A785 S55 2002
811'6-dc21   2002019286

Cover and text design by Random Features Industries

First Edition

Printed in the United States of America

CavanKerry Press Ltd.
Fort Lee, New Jersey
East Hampton, New York
www.cavankerrypress.com

for Ira
and our seven blessings,
Lauren, Amy, Gregg, Mark, Sarah, Ben and Nick

Family Chronology

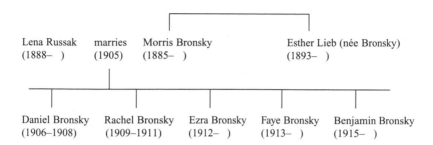

Lena Russak   marries   Morris Bronsky   Esther Lieb (née Bronsky)
(1888–)   (1905)   (1885–)   (1893–)

Daniel Bronsky   Rachel Bronsky   Ezra Bronsky   Faye Bronsky   Benjamin Bronsky
(1906–1908)   (1909–1911)   (1912–)   (1913–)   (1915–)

A Note from the Author

These connected poems tell the story of the Bronskys, a Jewish immigrant family of five living in Paterson, New Jersey, in the early twentieth century. The central voice is that of Faye Bronsky, a teenage girl whose life is disrupted by her mother's mental illness. Other voices include those of Faye's mother, Lena, who fled to Poland after her family perished in the Russian pogroms, then watched her first two children die of disease; and Faye's father, Morris, a silk weaver and loomfixer born in Poland, now actively involved in the struggle for workers' rights. During this period, Paterson, the silk capital of the country, was a center of radical unionism. While the personal lives of these characters are invented, historical figures, actual events, songs, and speeches have been used to convey the public and private atmosphere of this turbulent time in America.

CONTENTS

Knotted Threads

Fringed Babushka

Silk Weavings

The Language of Silk

FOREWORD

For Sondra Gash, silk is the fabric of memory. Strands of silk, sensuous but slippery, provide for Gash the brilliant but elusive substance of human relationships, especially as those relationships evolve in various places, and over time. Through the years these strands weave the tapestry of history and economics, and the human figures in those relationships both shine, and are caught, in silk's web.

But none of this will Sondra Gash tell you directly. Instead, she creates poems in the voices of adolescent Faye Bronsky, Faye's mother, Lena Russak, and her father, Morris Bronsky. These characters speak from one of the destinations on the silk trail, also a destination in the Jewish diaspora: the silk mill town of Paterson, New Jersey. The Bronskys have fled the old world of pogroms and European sensibilities and sensuousness for a new world of factories and difficult, sometimes fractured, freedom.

As he walks to work with the lunchbox his daughter has packed for him, Morris Bronsky speaks of unionizing these factories. Lena rhapsodizes from the unmoored mental states that cause her to confuse her life as a wife and mother with memories of her girlhood in Lodz, Poland. And Faye, the sun around whom these voices revolve, speaks plainly from the wisdom of her newly evolving womanhood. Though Morris manufactures silk, and Lena embroiders silk with her fantasies, it the honest, thoroughly unfrivolous, least silk-like Faye who shines. Neither tough as her father nor sensuous as her mother, Faye conscientiously picks up the strands of their threads and begins to weave a girl's own life in this new world.

It is a feat of ventriloquism for this poet to have developed such three-dimensional, utterly vital, characters' voices, as well as a host of minor ones, ranging from Faye's younger brothers to her aunt. To speak as these characters is one thing (they are loosely modeled after people in Gash's own family), but to make the poems that each of them would speak is quite another. It is the accomplishment of *Silk Elegy* that Sondra Gash suppresses her own contemporary style as a poet to write the poems of these characters, terse and direct in the case of Faye, stoutly narrative in the case of Morris, and romantic in the case of Lena. And these characters not only speak the poems of their interior lives, but create connections for a family saga that unravels: Lena's descent into mental illness, her stay at a sanatorium, and Faye's shouldering of the burden of her mother's absence with fear, anger, grace, and guts. They all survive. Lena returns; Morris has his wife again, as well as a daughter he encourages and admires; and Faye grows up.

Silk Elegy is the story of a family fabric that is almost rent in half and its rescuing restoration, not through miracles, but through steadiness of human connection — the human weave. Gash always keeps in mind a larger story, that of the history of anti-Semitism that brings the Bronskys to Paterson, and of the beginnings of the labor movement that was to hold the silk industry accountable for its workers. This book is not a collection of poems, but a single poem, standing on the integrity of its parts, just as individuals' integrities create a social fabric. Gash never abandons the metaphors of weaving, unweaving, and reweaving. They are endlessly useful and potent in her poet-as-storyteller's art.

Silk is Gash's "wine-dark sea," the metaphor that Homer weaves and reweaves to structure his telling of the *Odyssey*. But now, Odysseus is a teenage girl in Paterson. And her journey is to a schoolroom — and to a home which she must make, for her mother is on a shadow-Odyssey, to the dream-world of her own forsaken childhood. It is a measure of their tenacity that both these heroines return, and a measure of Gash's gift as a poet that she portrays them in images and lines as taut but voluptuous as the cloth which has caused them both to come so far.

Molly Peacock
Toronto and New York

Silk Elegy

now the river is still
no boats   no soaring birds

no churning wheels
down a path

into the injured heart
rows of bars

chain link fences
guarding vacant lots

on Market Street
in the museum

silk locked under glass
kimonos and shawls

mandarin coats
with cut iron sleeves

Paterson jacquard
ribbon and lace

the history of silk
pinned to the wall

along Spruce
up near the Falls

boarded windows
empty mills

no thread   no spools
no whirring looms

a faded sign
Silk City Dyeing

A TURBAN OF HANDKERCHIEFS

FAYE

Dawn, 1927

Mornings I wake to the moan
of the whistle. 6 A.M., my signal —
the nightshift is over.

Downtown, the weavers
turn off lights at their looms.
Papa closes his tool chest

and climbs up Hill Street,
his lunchpail swinging.
I know his path —

along the curve of the river,
past the mills
and the steady roar of the Falls.

He stops on the corner for milk
and the warm seeded rolls
he always brings home.

Mornings while Mama
and the boys
are still sleeping,

I wrap my robe around me
and stand at the window
watching light slowly unravel.

FAYE

A Turban of Handkerchiefs

all the time
Mama's headaches

she lives under turbans
I help her wrap them

hot wet handkerchiefs
rolled and twisted

a wobbly crown
on her head

in her bedroom
day folds into night

even at noon
Mama hides under the covers

shh   close the door
I need quiet

pull down the shades
I need dark

but even the quiet
not quiet enough

even the dark
not dark enough

FAYE

Every Night, Argument

The knot that holds them.
Papa tries to read,
hides inside the paper.
Mama flies at him,
I need someone to talk to.
You never stop, Lena.
She pulls off his glasses
and throws down the *Forward*.
He gets up to leave.

I bake — *mandelbrot,*
honey cake — keep my mind
on mixing dough
but my stomach churns.
Papa can fix
the iron and the clock —
but not Mama —
fevers, chills, thoughts
that will not go away.

On her table, pill bottles
stand at attention like my
brother Ben's toy soldiers.
When Mama's hot,
Papa opens windows.
When she's cold, he stokes
the coals. I go with him
to the cellar, his face flushed,
his shirtsleeves rolled.

FAYE

On the Curb

Sometimes I find her
stretched out on the curb.
She talks to strangers,

rolls down her thick lisle stockings,
Look at my purple veins,
so splotched and knotted.

On the boat crossing over
we buried Daniel, our first born.
Then, here, our little Rachel.

She must be so cold
in that tiny coffin
wearing such a thin nightshirt.

Have you seen her?
Ah, look who's here,
my girl Faye.

I take Mama home.
Papa says her loose-fitted soul
won't stay in its socket.

MORRIS

Shave Your Head, Put On a Sheitel

Yemenite girl I called her,
the prettiest girl in Pabianice.
Curls shiny as coal down to her waist.

Shave your head, Lena, put on a sheitel!
Before we married the rabbi tried
to convince her but she refused.

She would not wear a wig.
She wanted to leave behind
sidelocks and *sheitels.*

She wanted the New World.
I dreamed too. I could weave and fix looms.
We'd heard of Silk City

but what did I know. I thought
there were no sweatshops here.
No cockroach shops.

MORRIS

We Dreamed America

And finally we left.
From Lodz, a train
to Stettin, then a ship
bound for New York.
It was cold and windy
in the big open pit
called steerage.

The trip took weeks.
On the fourth day
Daniel coughed.
He ran a fever. All
night Lena held him
but by dawn he grew
limp in her arms.

She lay down on the deck
with him and wailed,
Make a casket for Daniel.
So I lined a crate
with her woolen shawl
and we buried
our boy in the sea.

Blackberry Tea

Lena was still a girl when
we arrived but she already
wore the turban of handkerchiefs.

When Rachel died
she climbed into bed
and dreamed backward.

She wanted her mother,
Podgorny Street,
the hills of Odessa.

I brought her blackberry tea
in a glass with a silver holder
the way she likes it,

a velvet hat braided with gold.
But she lay her head
on the pillow and cried,

I was born in Odessa
on the Black Sea.
I want to go back.

FAYE

Sleep

Papa works the night shift.
By day he sleeps on a cot in the room
he shares with Ezra and Ben.
It smells of mothballs.

Propped high on goosedown pillows,
Mama sleeps on her carved walnut bed.
Each night I tuck in the sheets
and lie on the sofa.

Poor Mama! Her nightmares
won't go away. Sometimes
she thinks she's a bird.
She glides through the house

flapping her arms in the dark,
Faye, did you know I could fly?
Come touch my feathers.
Look, I have wings!

FAYE

Dancing with Gypsies

A hot summer night on the porch,
the only sounds the shy squeak of the glider,
fireflies tapping the screen.
Mama rocks back and forth,
a halter dress pulled up on her thighs,
stockings rolled to her ankles.

When I was young, she croons,
I danced with gypsies on the hills of Odessa.
The boys wore silk pantaloons,
the girls, gauze skirts with tiny mirrors
stitched into the cloth
indigo   saffron   magenta!

A boy with dusky eyes sat on the riverbank
strumming a mandolin. I came near.
He touched my cheek.
Your skin's like silk, he said.
His name was Majik.

Mama stares at the trees,
then starts to sing:
tum ba la   tum ba la
tum ba la laika
tum ba la   tum ba la
tum ba la laika…

A breeze climbs to the fourth floor
grazing my seersucker gown.
She spritzes seltzer from the cloud blue bottle.
Faye, marry someone who will lift you,
let you breathe beneath the covers!

M. Russak and Sons, We Make Suits
— Odessa, 1898

In the front room of the house on Podgorny,
bolts of wool lined the walls,
on the floor, swatches of flannel,
tweed, gabardine.

Tateh sat near the window
bent over the sewing machine,
a silk cap on his head,
a glass of schnapps by his side.

In the tawny light he looked like
the man in the Rembrandt painting —
dark beard, whiskers, grave bushy brows.
Wire-rimmed glasses slid down his nose.

When customers arrived for fittings,
he shooed me to the back,
but when he worked alone
he liked me nearby.

He taught me to sew — men's coat buttons
with heavy thread and thimble.
We'd loop a needle back and forth.
He let me press pleats.

I liked the moist smell of wool,
heat steaming up through the iron,
men's suits, men's voices,
the heft of their bodies.

I went with him to the gypsy camp
where he bought cloth from a horse-
drawn wagon. Next morning,
he made me a vest with a red silk lining.

FAYE

Singed Goosefeathers

I was ten when she locked the door, took the key
and left me in the house with Ben and Ezra.

I'm supposed to watch my brothers.
They run wild all over the house,
looking for pennies. They lift Mama's
mattress. It's dark. Ben lights a candle.

Sparks shoot up, smoke curls in the room.
Faye, come quick, Ezra screams.
We grab pillows to smother the flames
but it's too late — they're leaping wildly,

the air's caught fire! We run to the kitchen —
the window's stuck. I break the glass
with a pot. The metal steps shudder
as we race down the fire escape.

Neighbors pour out of the building.
Ben's crying, my body's shaking.
Ezra is holding our hands.
Fire engines clang onto the street.

Firemen set up ladders. *Where's your*
Mama? they call as they climb
to the fourth floor with their hoses,
Where's your Mama?

For weeks, the burning stench,
singed goosefeathers stuck to the walls.

FAYE

Seven

At midnight propped high on goosedown pillows,
she reads from the Book of Splendor.
I must unravel secrets, I've had
hints from above, she murmurs.
Wrapped in a flowered kimono,
the crepe paper bird on her head —
Mama, all dressed up for dreaming!

In Kabbala, seven's the magic number —
seven blessings, seven seas, seven pillars
of wisdom. The bride circles her groom
seven times. The rebbes dance seven rings
around clay when they shape the golem.
We'll all pass seven spheres
before we reach seventh heaven.

Mama's stories! The stars that followed her
to school at dawn, the palace of pearls
on the mountain top, moon men
gliding over tile roofs, pickled
herring, thrones of black kasha,
reclining zaddiks and
green mandolins.

Mama's stories! Papa calls them inventions.
They spill like beads across the floor.
Sometimes she tries cures — eucalyptus,
rose hip tea, fish oil emulsion.
Alone in her room she chants
holding her healing stones —
crystal, jade, agate.

Is there a cure for dreaming?
At Rachel's grave she dances.
At the lake in the country
she takes off her robe, slips
into the deep. *I'm a fish,*
she sings and her voice
rises over the water.

FAYE

I Bring Papa's Lunch to Lambert's Mill

On the plank floor of the weave room,
clack of wooden shuttles, clash
of wheels and gears pulling looms,

men in white shirts, suspenders,
dark gabardine, women in black,
high-collared muslin.

Shafts fly up and down, spindles whir.
I find Papa, his wiry arms always
moving — just like the machines.

A bobbin slips off the yarn,
a shuttle jams. He lifts
a wrench from his toolchest,

bends forward and the loom
rides again, back and forth,
back and forth over the threads.

I watch Papa's hands,
small, quick, a mesh of lines
tattooed on his palms.

FAYE

Sundays Papa Comes Home Late

He pulls on his woolly sweater,
the one from Poland
with strange curly buttons.

I set his bowl in its place
at the table: boiled chicken,
carrots, *kneidlach* and soup.

Again the Workmen's Circle,
Mama snaps, *all day playing cards,*
talking union. I know you gamble.

Lena, everything I earn is for you
and the children. God forbid
they end up in the mills…

Faye should go to high school.
We let Ezra go.
She's the one with all A's.

Girls are different, Mama cries,
I need her at home.
Let Esther help you.

Your sister talks too much. I want Faye.
Papa's head droops over the bowl.
His shoulders sag.

FAYE

The Key

She tries to knock me down but
I know where she keeps it hidden
so I reach inside her nightgown,
twist her arm, slip in and take it —
a warm jewel pressed between
her big breasts. I rush to the door
and unlock it, her voice chasing
me as I race down four flights.

Faye, come back, you're crazy.

No, Mama, I whisper, not crazy yet.
Her shrieks blaze in my head as I run —
past the empty lot on the corner,
past Duman's Market and Freed's
Luncheonette. I'm still wearing
my apron but I can't stop. It's the
first day of school and I'm going!

Wind fills my chest. I feel light.
My arms whirl up and back like the
rolling ovals of the Palmer Method
we learned in third grade. All the way
the key is tight in my fist. Then
I'm standing outside the school,
a ship with rows of tall windows.
I untie my apron, tuck the key into my
pocket and walk through the front door.

FAYE

School Auditorium, First Day at Westside High

We're in the assembly
singing the Star-Spangled Banner
when she opens the door and cries out,

Fayela, school's not for girls.
I need you at home!

Heads turn, voices stop.
The velvet curtain
sways on the stage.

Mama, wearing the handkerchief
turban and Papa's coat
over her nightgown,

totters down the aisle
calling out vows
like a wind-up bride,

I want you, Faye.
I want you at home.

The girls near me giggle,
my teacher glares,
I swing around,

stumble over feet in my row,
take Mama's hand
and lead her up the aisle,

whispering, Shh, Mama,
shh, we're leaving.
We're going home.

FAYE

Cohen's Dry Goods

Mama's well enough
to climb out of bed
and find me a job —
Cohen's Dry Goods
on the corner
of Weaver and Hill.

Silk sold by the yard for a dime!
buttons and beads
grommets and snaps
bolts of calico
rolled out
under the rotating fan
moiré   pinwale   chambray

I'm good with my hands like Papa.
I measure and cut
learn to stitch
seed pearls into a bodice
white *peau de soie.*

In the back room
Mr. Cohen chalks hems.
He teaches me
buttonholes, zippers.
Now Ezra's a sophomore.
He's learning history.

FAYE

My History Lessons

i.   The Silk Road

In Shantung in 2640 B.C.
the Princess Hsi Ling Shi
sat in her garden
under a mulberry tree.
When something fell into
her cup, she unraveled
a long shining thread.

> Her ladies-in-waiting found
> cocoons high in the branches.
> Holding bowls in their laps
> they plucked and unwound.
> *We'll call this silk,* the Princess
> said, *and keep it a secret.*

Silk, for centuries only in China,
death the penalty for stealing
larvae or seeds.

> Silk, piled high on camels,
> caravans crossing the Silk Road,
> past mountains and deserts,
> Mongols and thieves.

But one day two monks
smuggled seeds and larvae
in hollowed canes,
took them to Damascus,
Rome, Constantinople!

ii.   Paterson

In 1791, Acquackanonk on the Passaic —
a sleepy village — ten houses, a tavern,
Main Street called Peace and Plenty Lane.

The patriarch Hamilton saw the river.
He heard the roar of the Falls
and he dreamed —

> *here in this valley*
> *beneath wooded hills*
> *we'll build raceways and dams*
> *locomotives and looms*
> *a cradle of industry*
> *a city of mills*

Immigrants arrived from Palermo,
Dublin, Manchester, Lodz,
silk giving shape to their lives.

> the dyer dipped skeins into vats
> the reeler lifted threads
> the winder rolled strands
> onto spools

Satin   taffeta   jersey   moiré
Industrial silk!

> all day   all night
> the taste of dust
> the clash of wheels pulling looms
> headle and shunt
> bobbin and reel
> spindle and reel

Paterson, iron fist in a sleeve of silk.

UNRAVELING

FAYE

What Is Wrong with Mama?

Papa calls her *luftmensch.*
Aunt Esther says she has spells.
Neighbors whisper *meshuga.*
At four A.M. she stands in the parlor
holding a can of *Bon Ami.*
Shine the tub, Faye, scrub the floor.

What is wrong with Mama?
She hisses when she finds
a smudge on the wall, then sinks
for hours into the darkest place.
Today, she says, *the woman*
inside me is hiding her face.

What is wrong with Mama?
She quivers on one side, roars
on the other. Her mind zigzags
like the stitches the Singer makes.
Words burst like steam from the pot.
And the voices.

Who does she see in the mirror
when the woman inside
hides her face?

ESTHER

I Tell Faye Lena's Story

Faye, the Cossacks stormed
through the shtetl and murdered
your Mama's whole family.

She walked alone across mountains,
an orphan girl searching for cousins.
When Rachel died,

your Mama roamed dark
streets. One night she stood
at my door and moaned…

There is no stone for Ima,
her body's engraved in fire.
Tateh's bones are shaped by wind.

My brothers too, burned to ash.
We buried Daniel, our first born
on the boat coming over.

We let his casket sink into the sea.
Now where is my Rachel,
my girl who waved to the moon?

The Silk Strike of 1913

The mills were damp and caked with grime.
Cockroaches scurried over the floors.
In the dyeshops steam so thick
we could not see our fingers.

The mills were fire traps, the doors
always locked. We could not leave
our looms without permission,
not even for the bathroom.

We were immigrants from Manchester,
Dublin, Palermo, Lodz — loom-
fixers, weavers, dyers, winders,
23,000 men, women and children.

There were strikes all over.
Ours one of the largest —
Barbour Thread, Lambert's Mill,
Doherty Silk and hundreds more.

We wanted safe conditions,
an eight-hour day and no child labor.
The owners wanted to assign us
more looms and cut back our pay

so we marched up Main Street
holding up placards:
IF THE OWNERS WANT SILK
LET THEM WEAVE IT THEMSELVES!

FAYE

He Was a Bobbin Boy When He Was Eight

Sometimes on Sundays I walk with Papa
past Mama's dark room,
past Woolworth's, the Rivoli,
the markets and mills
and he starts to talk…

I was a bobbin boy when I was eight.
Lodz was a silk city too —
there were blocks and blocks of mills —
for dyeing, printing and weaving.

Each building had its own whistle,
its rows of pulleys, belts, rollers,
chains. The Silk Works! Shipping docks,
loading zones, warehouses, trucks.

We lived right there behind sooty windows
in workers' flats hemmed in by the dark.
They paid us in script. We had to buy
food and supplies from the company store.

Papa sighs and we stop on the bridge
to look down at the river —
so clear we can see minnows jumping.
Then across Market,

up Spruce to McBride on old
crooked sidewalks 'til we reach
the footpath high over the Falls
where we can breathe light.

FAYE

Her Hats

I see them sailing up Broadway
over chimneys and trees, high
into the clouds — the velvet cloche,
the red beret, the floppy velour.

I see them perched like sparrows
on wires overhead. Her crazy hats —
the crepe paper bird,
the handkerchief turban,

the sequinned crown, the ones
she finds in used clothing stores,
the ones she makes with fishnet,
feather, cardboard and string.

When I open windows,
they flutter, nod, daven and soar.
They stream out in space
like Mama who says she can fly.

Mama, I want to shout, let geese
flap their wings, let milkweed
glide through the sky —
you belong here on earth with us.

But when I ask her why she needs
so many hats, she tips
her lace fedora and says,
because I have so many heads!

FAYE

Alta Kop

The open market on Summer
and Park, a white tile floor
sprinkled with sawdust,
barrels of apples and plums.

I squeeze lightly,
put back the bruised ones,
choose deep purple eggplant,
string beans that snap.

Papa says I have an *alta kop.*
No sprouted onions,
no green potatoes.
At closing time,

I find bargains, half-price
bananas, ripe tomatoes.
The produce man
pulls down a string of garlic

from a rope on the ceiling,
*Schena meidela, this is for you
and your Mama.* I walk home with my
necklace of cloves.

Russians hang cloves of garlic from doors
and windows to ward off evil.

Garlic brings back the soul to a sick person.

— *Encyclopaedia of Superstitions
and Folklore*

FAYE

The Trolley

I want to cry when she climbs aboard —
the purple socks, the red babushka,
the gauze dress — patched pockets
and ballooning sleeves — sad scraps
sewn together and Mama muttering.

I wish I could hide. Those girls
in the back — they knew me in school.
They'll laugh — her gypsy beads,
shiny cheeks, circles of rouge
she never bothers to blend.

And she talks to strangers.
I shrink down and pray,
Please God, don't let her see me!

FAYE

Jane Eyre

When I unlock the door
and open Cohen's shop
sunlight pours through the windows.

I like the reddish glow of the floorboards,
the whirring fan on the ceiling,
a rainbow of spools lined up in rows.

It's so quiet. I can read before
customers come. It used to be like this
at home. Sunny and peaceful.

I played library before anyone woke,
my desk, the parlor bench.
Papa made me shelves out of crates.

I collected old books from neighbors,
lined them in rows, wrote little notes
on squares of white paper:

*This book is about a boy caught
in a storm. This one's about
a girl who saves a baby.*

It used to be like this at home.
Sunny and peaceful. A long time ago
before Mama got sick.

Now I sit on the stool
behind the marble counter
and open *Jane Eyre*.

LENA

Pogrom, Odessa, 1898

Just as I stepped onto Pushkin Square
holding a tin of milk, a basket of eggs,
Cossacks on horseback swept by firing guns.
Crowds began screaming and running.
I dropped to the ground, eggs splattering my coat.

Two feet away, an old man fell.
Blood spilled in a puddle around him.
Oh God, a woman wailed, *they've shot
the Rebbe.* The baker's wife grabbed my hand,
Come, meidela, we'll find your Mama.

No, I want to go home, I whispered,
I want to go home. My lips pressed tight, I raced
down Tolskya Street clutching the empty tin.
Inside I wound gauze around my bleeding knees
and hid under the bed.

I couldn't move. I couldn't speak.
Ima cried when she found me, *Lena, we looked
everywhere for you.* All night she held me
wrapped in her quilt. All night guns roared,
shadows crawled over the walls.

FAYE

The Library Book

At the sink drying dishes, I prop
my book against the back wall,
careful not to splash the pages.

Mama comes flying,
her hair in wild tufts,
her cheeks ablaze.

I drop the towel on the book.
Don't try to hide that, she shouts,
snatching *Jane Eyre.*

She twists a piece of thick
brown paper into a cone
and lights a burner at the stove.

Mama, that's not yours, you can't!
Oh, no? she screams,
sweeping the burning cone

over the book. I grab her arm
but she shoves me aside.
The flames catch,

the pages turn black and shrivel.
Jane Eyre lies in the sink,
smoldering.

My Golem

They called me a sleepwalker.
One night in the graveyard I danced in circles over stones
and she came to me, a woman of clay. Did I dream her?
No, my hands shaped the clay: a torso, arms and legs.
I smoothed her brow, etched magic words on her forehead.

She was not a giant like the golems
created by men but she had a voice and I listened: *You come
from a long line of rhapsodic women,* she whispered. I kept
her a secret. Behind my bedroom door, she tried on my lace fedora
and filigree gloves.

But she needed clothes as I did
when we arrived. We came here with nothing. When Rachel died,
I could not speak the language. Now I had a friend to talk to.
I bought her a chemise and a matching cape finished with braid.
I'm an American woman now, she said to the mirror.

It was her idea to buy the hats.
They spilled over closets, a velvet cloche, a red beret, a straw
trimmed with ribbons that streamed out in space but she wanted
more. She grew so wild I used a stickpin to hold down her
head. You're too much for this world, I shouted.

She whirled into the kitchen
and set Faye's book on fire. *I don't fit in,* she cried, interrupting
my heartbeat. She'd been a sister to me. Together we'd laughed
and cried. I took her back to the graveyard, read aloud from
the Zohar, blessed her seven times over a candle.

The holy words melted. My golem
fell. I draped her with my shawl. I'm not sleeping now, you know.
Everything's begun to fall. I wear my hair down to my waist.
My broken beads lie on the floor. In the dark,
I chant backward prayers.

FAYE

Nightmare

Not a star in the sky.
And the moon is hiding.
I lie in a coffin,

Mama hunched over me
in the black robe of her wings.
I try to stand.

You can't rise from a coffin,
she squawks and bangs
down the lid. Mama, I cry,

don't bury me
but she flaps her wings,
then she's off in the air —

I can fly, Faye, I can fly!

FAYE

The Library

As I walk along Broadway,
my face burns, wind tugs my hair.
Shadows fall over windows.

Will they still let me borrow books?
I can't explain, can't say
my mother set *Jane Eyre* on fire.

I stare at the wide stone columns.
The Public Library! I've been
coming here since I was small.

I love the cool marble,
quiet books lined up in rows.
Even before I could read

I'd sit at the long pine table
and let my fingertip
trail down the lines of print.

Once at closing time
I lay my head down
and dreamed this was my home.

Now I climb the stairs,
afraid to open
the carved wooden door.

FAYE

Mama's the Fire

Now I hide the books
under the pillow
where she never looks.
When she goes to bed
I read on the sofa.

Nothing's mine in this house.
Not even the place
where I sleep. She takes
my pay for her pills
and hats. She thinks

she can burn a book
she doesn't own. Mama's
the fire that sweeps
over everything. But
last night in my dream

when she tried to push me
into the flames, they
leaped up around her.
Last night in my dream
I watched Mama burn.

FAYE

I'm Papa's Girl

He takes me with him,
holds my hand on the train.
We sway over bridges,
around tracks and bends.
I lean against him
until we are there.

Coney Island in hazy August,
the beach, the broiling sun,
the hiss and boom of waves.
Papa's green visored cap,
his striped canvas chair
sunk in the sand.

I swim out far — long strokes
into the swells. I could drift
like this forever. I could
reach the horizon,
nothing holding me
but the sea.

Back home late at night,
heat drones
over drooping trees.
Ezra and Ben
sprawl on their cots,
each tangled in sheets.

Alone on the porch
Mama glides
back and forth,
back and forth,
cooling off in the dark,
and her head whirs like a loom.

FAYE

Now All the Time She Hears Voices

I find her on the fire escape
in a sheer nightgown.
Mama, come inside, it's cold.

Her eyes are glassy,
her lips move without sound
but she takes my hand.

Something's snapped
like thread on the bobbin.
Papa has to take her away.

A raw day in November.
He holds the suitcase.
She's buttoned her coat wrong.

These are for you, Faye,
she says, and she gives me
her box of healing stones.

Please keep my secrets.
Shh, Papa says. He takes her arm.
I plant a kiss on her cheek,

fix her buttons
and watch from the stoop.
Small puffs of breath

float in the air
as he steers her along.
They disappear.

Can we visit? What is an asylum?

KNOTTED THREADS

His Dark Song

This is the longest night.
Not one shred of sleep.
Each of us breathing
in our separate beds.
Each of us wrapped
in our own spool
of darkness.

Her Dark Song

This is the longest night.
Only the knot of the dark
twisting around me.
Only the night river
winding. Grief
sits on my head
like a crow.

FAYE

I Overhear

Neighbors down the hall:

> *They sent away the crazy lady in 20A.*
> *The daughter cooks and cleans*
> *for her father and brothers.*
> *And she has a job.*
> *Poor thing, she's just a girl.*

Papa in the parlor:

> *Faye's always been grown up.*
> *When she was six she brought*
> *Lena meals in bed and she stood*
> *on a stool to boil soup for Ben.*

Aunt Esther:

> *Poor thing, she's just a girl.*

FAYE

Fire and Water

Now I come to the river,
stand on the footbridge
high above the Falls,
letting spray wet my face,
watching white shooting
foam crash below.
All this rumbling
drowns out Mama's cries.

But suddenly mists
turn the air milky gray
and I hear a voice,
Come with me, Faye,
come into the river.
Is that you, Mama,
climbing the rock wall?
Is that your cape
or the moss that clings
to the ledge?

Again I hear her call,
Turn with the river, Faye.
Then I'm inside
the torrent, tumbling.
The river fills me.
I am the river plunging
into deep pools of light.
Mama, don't perch
on the cliff. Please,
Mama, don't fall.
But a flood of sunlight
burns over the water
and Mama is gone.

My Brother Ben

He lies, he brags, he opens drawers and takes nickels.
Last week the truant officer knocked on our door,
All week your brother Ben's been playing hookey.

I know where he goes — to Freed's Luncheonette
where he bets on pinball machines.
Today Mr. Freed told me,

Your brother Ben's been stealing —
cigarettes, Hershey bars, halvah.
I told him, next time I'll call the police.

He's always been wild. He's the one who set
Mama's room on fire. I try to warn him —
Ben, if you don't stop, you'll end up in jail.

I'll be rich someday, he says,
I'm not like Papa — I won't work for pennies.
I'll go to New York,

buy a thousand balloons for a dime
and sell them for a penny each.
Someday, you'll see, I'll be king of the mills!

FAYE

Girl with Laundry Basket

In her backyard near the river
a girl is pinning clothes to a line.
As she pulls the cord through the pulley,
her sheets climb over rooflines
like ghost-dancers whirling.

She lifts a shirt from her basket,
stops to look up at the boat on the river
and I wonder if she ever dreams
of sailing, the light blue
and wide rising inside her.

I've seen her before. I think I know her —
a girl wearing an apron
and a red bandana like mine.
I'll call her sister.
I'll call her Rachel.

FAYE

The Way He Ran, I Thought He Was a God

My brother Ezra, out on the oval track,
wiry legs, arms pumping air.
He flashes by in morning light, his feet
the wings of some god I saw
in Mama's book of myths.

My brother Ezra makes me dizzy —
the way he speeds through space —
spiked shoes, green satin shorts,
face glistening with sweat.
I have to shield my eyes.

He'll win the race.
I'll look through the glass
and see his medals shining
in a case at Westside High
for all the world to see.

My brother Ezra.
I look up and he's coming round
the bend, spinning like a comet
round the sun. Here he is.
Here he is again.

ESTHER

Berliner Coats

Deep woods surrounded Pabianice.
Everything heavy and cold — dark stone,
a root cellar, thick black boots in the snow.
I wanted romance so I came to New York
but it was just as cold here. I lived with
cousins in a cold water flat, carried my
sewing machine on my back.

My first job. Berliner Coats.
Treadles buzzing, feet pedalling,
a hundred women lined up in rows.
The first day I'm stitching a sleeve
when the girl beside me slumps down
and falls in a heap to the floor.

I jump up like a jack-in-the-box,
loosen her shirtwaist and untie
the stays of her corset. I get her to stir,
rip open the orange in my sack
and squirt juice straight into her mouth.

Miss Bronsky, the foreman shouts,
Get back to your machine or you're fired!
But this girl's fainted. *She's faking,*
he says. I'll take her home, I say.
If you leave, don't come back.

That was my last day at Berliner Coats.
After that, I learned to weave.
But it was just as bad.
No talking allowed and no sitting.

No room for mistakes.
Every morning I wound my hair
into a braid and swept it up into a bun.
I could not let one strand
get caught in the loom.

FAYE

Papa Takes Me to a Meeting

Up creaky stairs over a store,
a smoke-filled hall, clackety chairs.
From a shaky platform, a speaker shouts,

Can we strike for fair wages?
Are we for an eight-hour day?

Clenched fists punch the air.
Men, women, even children cry out,
We can fight, we can win!

A man near us waves his hand —
the color of blood. I look at Papa.
From the dye, he says.

After the vote, cheers roar
through the hall. Then what I like best,
the crowd bursts into song…

When the union's inspiration
through the workers' blood shall run,

there can be no power greater
anywhere beneath the sun…

Solidarity forever, solidarity forever,
for the union makes us strong.

At home, Papa pins up a picture
of Eugene V. Debs on the wall.

FAYE

Blue Silk

Late at night in the quiet,
pins pressed in my mouth,
I lay tissue over blue silk,

smooth out the wrinkles,
check the pattern once more
before I start to cut.

This style is new —
a dress with raglan sleeves
and a jeweled neckline.

I thread the needle,
wind the bobbin,
stitch front to back,

making sure the notches
match. The treadle buzzes,
my fingers guide cloth,

a naked bulb burns overhead.
For years I've unraveled
hems in Mama's skirts,

lengthened pants
for Ezra and Ben,
darned Papa's socks.

Now piece by piece,
I've tucked them away.
This blue silk is for me!

FAYE

The Visit

When Papa says we can go
I press shirts for the boys.
At dawn the bus winds
along back country roads,
leaves swirl in the air.
How will she be?
What should we say?

In the hall a patient leaps at us,
her arms sweeping wildly.
Two others are strapped
in chairs. A woman with
a blank face suddenly hisses.

Mama looks frail in a thin
cotton dress. Papa holds her
for a long time. Ben gives her a hug.
You need new shoes, she cries.
Ezra takes her hand. She gives
him a slice of stale bread.

Those are her boys, her boys,
her roommate says.
Mama nods, *Yes, my boys.*
Does she see me? She comes close.
Her hair brushes my cheek.
She slips a string of crepe
paper beads over my head.
Fayela, I made these for you.

FAYE

Mama's Room

This is Mama's room — the vanity
where she rolls her hair
into two curving pompadours
Papa calls horns!

This is where she whispered,
Sit down, my little Russke,
I'll make you beautiful.
I watched in the mirror

as she combed my dark curls,
dabbed rouge on my cheeks,
kohl on my eyes. *When I was a girl,*
my hair curled to my waist.

This is Mama's room — in her
chifforobe, the moiré dress
I wore at Aunt Esther's wedding,
its sleeves still puffed with tissue.

I turn back the covers
and sit on her bed.
I could sleep here but I'm afraid
I'll sink into her sadness.

FAYE

Nightshift

Asleep in his armchair,
Papa doesn't hear when I call.
The Evening News lies on the floor.
Through the loose weave of his shirt
I see the grey hairs on his chest.
Is he old? His face looks worn
as the cushion nap. Seams
line his cheeks. Is he sick?
I hear him wheeze in his sleep.

All that lint dust at the mill.
And the noisy shuttles don't stop.
He plugs his ears with cotton.
Did he come here from Poland
to work the nightshift?
The graveyard shift they call it.
I tap his shoulder. *Papa,*
it's time to wake up.

FAYE

First Grade

When Papa called from the street
I ran to the window.
He stood on the sidewalk
holding his hat like a beggar.
Go tell Mama I need a handout!

I threw down three pennies.
He caught them, one at a time,
shuffled, bowed and hurried
off to the corner store
for the paper.

Five minutes later,
he rushed up the stairs
and whirled me around.
Are you set for school?
Yes, Papa, I can't wait.
What's that in the box?

And he gave me the gift —
a plaid bookbag with real
leather straps and my name
printed on the front in gold.
Inside: a yellow pad, a pencil
box, a sharpener that spewed
tiny curls of wood.

Papa put on his glasses
and turned to *The World*.
I sat on the floor
with a new sheet of paper
and began to practice my words.

Bread and Roses

"Paterson Police Chase and Club Strikers.
Bar Thousands From Meeting."
— *Paterson News,* February 1913

Every Sunday all through that winter
we gathered next door in Haledon —
23,000 strikers huddled for hours
on a field outside the home of a
weaver named Botto. John Reed,
Emma Goldman and the Wobblies —
Bill Haywood, Gurley Flynn, Carlo
Tresca — stood on the balcony, shouting:

One big union. No more exploitation.
We want bread and we want roses!

The strike went on for months.
We were hungry and cold, our savings
gone. Some of us had to farm out
our children. The city's Cooperative
bakers donated loaves of pumpernickel
and seeded rye. Gifts poured in from
everywhere but the courts, the papers,
300 owners were all against us.

You're just workers. Morris. Give up.
There are no laws to protect you.
I didn't come here to be a slave, Lena.
If we stick together, we'll win.
String your big words on a line, they'll
just flap in the wind. She was right.
We lost and my boss Mr. Lambert
smiled down on us from his castle,
Bella Vista, 26 rooms on top of the hill.

Valentino Modestino, 1913

He was a man on a porch holding his baby.
We were a crowd of strikers
picketing outside Weidmann's plant.

It was a Saturday in April.
There were scabs, Pinkertons,
police waving billy clubs,

a detective blasting a gun in the air.
Poor Modestino. He just happened to be there.
This is amazing, he said when he fell.

Three days later we walked from the church
on East 19th Street to Laurel Grove.
It was raining, the sky black as iron.

People leaned over fences and stood
at their windows watching the long stream
of mourners pass by.

It was a funeral procession.
There were no carriages, there were no hearses,
there were no prayers.

We were just workers, thousands
of workers, each placing
a red carnation on the coffin.

I remember Modestino's baby, her blonde
curly hair. And the carnations, a blood red
mountain covering the grave.

Mama, I See You Everywhere

high on a treetop
draped in black feathers

circling the cliffs
in a purple crown

you swoop toward me
wearing the mask of a crow

in blue air you shimmer
your dark wings pull me in

when sleep covers windows
you shriek and wheel

Mama, you keep coming back
a loon on the river

a mourning dove
a white crane

perched on one leg
beneath the moon

FRINGED BABUSHKA

FAYE

The Compact

I find it rolled up in her nightgown,
glazed cloisonné, blackberries
etched on the lid.

Beneath the clasp
Mama's scented face powder
sprinkled over the mirror.

I clear a space with my finger
and she's here — in my cheeks,
my dark curls, the same eyes,

green as her jade healing stones.
Mama thinks she's in Odessa
but she's weaving dreams

in the asylum. She's told me
so many stories that sometimes
I think I've been there.

And so many times she's told me,
I come from a long line
of rhapsodic women.

LENA

My Escape

Dear Fayela,

Last night in my room
moonlight spilled through the bars,
feathers danced on the sill.
When I tried to touch them,
doves spread their wings
and flew into the sky.
Then I knew — they came
here to lead me. So I climbed
the ledge, lifted my arms
and soared with the birds.
I floated high above
the roofs of Vilna,
until at last I reached
the hills of Odessa!

Love and love again,

Mama

FAYE

In My Dream, Klezmer Music

Under a lapis moon, black-booted Cossacks
leap and kick, women in embroidered skirts
click their heels and whirl. Bagpipes,
violins, the low notes of an oboe
and the balalaika plays.

Suddenly Mama's on stage —
a girl in muslin dancing with gypsies
on a hill in Odessa. A shepherd's
flute echoes down mountain slopes
and I hear her song, the one she sings
on summer nights on the porch…

tum ba la tum ba la
tum ba la laika
tum ba la tum ba la
tum ba la laika

Then I'm with her in a café on Arbot Street.
She looks like the *matreshka* doll
on her dresser, head in a babushka,
cheeks rouged magenta. Spice tea
is served in a glass with a silver holder,
black currant bread.

Roving *klezmerim* are playing:
a clarinet, a little drum, a mandolin.
Are you well, Mama?
Yes, here I can dance!
She lifts her skirt and climbs
on the table the way she did
at Aunt Esther's wedding.

Dark-eyed men clap and throw kisses.
Then we all rise for the horah.
I'm still with her on ragged streets.
The *hazzan* is chanting. We are
flying over the roofs of the shtetl,
hiding under hay in a wagon.

Mama, you said we come from
a family of rhapsodic women
but never told me enough.
Hold my hand, Faye, we'll climb
the steep hills to the turn of the century.
You wear the carnelian
earrings I gave you.
I'll wear my beaded crown.

FAYE

Luftmensch, Sleepwalker, Loose-fitted Soul

When a full moon steals through the window,
I tiptoe into your room,
open the tortoise shell box.

Mama, you've left me your charms —
carnelian, amber, knotted jade
from the Palace of Czars.

All your locked pearls filled with the moon.
I slip on the coral necklace,
the onyx beads,

the long string of lapis
and wrapped in your healing stones,
I shine like you!

Mama, I've tried you on and you fit.
Now I'm the luftmensch,
sleepwalker, loose-fitted soul.

LENA/MORRIS

Asylum Conversation

My name is Russak,
I want it back.
I want the house with blue minarets.

> There's nothing left there, Lena,
> You fled Odessa when you were a girl.

Look through the window, Morris.
Ima is lifting a pear from the bowl,
holding it up to the light.
The pear is her jewel!

> Does she forget how her father
> hid her in a closet before the Cossacks
> set the family on fire?

> Does she forget how their cries
> burned through the windows?

> Do you know you're a Bronsky now,
> Lena? Do you know who I am?

Yes, Morris, you are my husband,
the warmth on the sill
when the sun goes down.

LENA

The Kosmos

Dear Faye,

       I'm camped here with gypsies.
They come from India, Mozambique, China,
in all shades of skin — carnelian, onyx, amber.
They speak in ragged tongues, waving the iridescent
flags of their lives. I'm wearing my beaded turban
and talking with anyone who will listen.

       A girl strolls along spilling flowers
from a wagon, a man in a wheelchair rolls by the *berioska*
and I just hugged a boy who might be my Daniel.
In the square, a woman plays a mandolin and sings
our song. But still I worry. The police are everywhere,
disguised in braided caftans and shawls.
Are you alone in the house with Ben?

       I want you to know I found
the lacquer spice box lost so long ago. Oh, Faye,
I'm waiting for you. I have a basket of eggs —
the cracked ones I always buy. Please hurry.
I'll make you a matzo brei. My address is:
Kosmos Hotel, 77 Levertov, Russia. Then
we'll fly on a Turkish rug to Podgorny Street.

Love and kisses, Mama

Love again, Mama

LENA

Dreaming Backward

Dear Morris,

        I'm still here at the Kosmos.
It's so crowded, people from near and far come and go,
women carry cargoes of grief on their heads. It is cold here.
It is winter. Ragmen sell beaver and astrakhan hats from pushcarts.

        Everything's jumbled — too much
excitement, too little sleep. After I fell in the grove, after I
threw out the pills, I came here. Don't worry. This place
has saved me. I'm alive and soon I'll be coming home.
But first I'm going to walk down the thousand steps to the sea.

        Here the light shines like enamel.
I know you think I'm sick. You say all this is in my mind.
But my feet are on the path with all the ruined ones. See
the petals fall beneath the tree. Three days old and already
blooming their hearts away.

        Ukrainian eggs sit on the table.
I can hear music, songs that hold seeds of the night, stories
that fill the white bowl of dreams. I hear the chord of the Kosmos.
Here I am alive. Not like this woman, my roommate from Minsk.
She wants to die. God slammed the door in her face. The stars
are my seeing eyes. They lead me through the dark.

I'm not dreaming backward. This is what happens. I write all the time but I don't mail the letters. Don't worry. Soon I'll be turning. I came here to say Kaddish for the old ones. And Morris, my patient husband, your callused hands, the way you savor my plum applesauce, I want to see you.

Please don't tell me I'm not here. See how I push the door open and enter the deep space of the Kosmos. See the moon, a pool of silver strands. There are leftover threads to be stitched.

I am almost turning.

Your Lena

LENA

On the Black Sea in Odessa

A ferry dreams through fog.
Women glide over cobblestone streets,
past alleys where light is so weary
it turns as they leave. Men cross
the square, arms folded behind them,
gabardine suits worn to a shine.
I know the ancient high-ceilinged shul,
everything yellowing: prayer books,
curtains, walls, smoky candle wax,
worn oak.

Oh, the buzz of voices as we climb
to the alcove to sit with the women.
Below us, a sea of yarmulkes,
men in fringed tallis, davenning.
Oh, their somber beards,
the serious suits waiting in closets
year after year, collars frayed.
The rabbi unlocks the Ark —
two Torah scrolls draped in velvet.
The *hazzan* wails, a deep tomb of song.

Beyond the leaded windows,
I know the women sweeping stoops,
their Khazar faces like mine.
I know the melodies — a Moldavian
folksong, a Yiddish lullaby,
echoes of AsiaMinsk.
I know the breezes that blow
in from the sea, over balconies,
under awnings, across the wide
embroidered skirts of Odessa.

LENA

Could This Be My Brother?

His cheeks ruddy,
his shape stocky and proud
like my father's.
He leads me to a small room,
a wall of books.
On the table, dark bread,
lingonberry jam.

Can we talk, I ask.
He shuts the window.
Heat simmers.
Sticky flypaper
curls from the ceiling.
They steal our books.
They don't let us breathe.
We pray by candlelight
in the cellar.

I want to bring him
home with me,
give him towels
aired in the sun,
a satin tallis for his shoulders,
a quiet room
where he can read.

LENA

Lost Amber

Come with me, Faye.
We'll take the night train
past fields of shimmering birch.
When light seeps through pale curtains,
we'll board a streetcar and ride
to the end of the line.

Come with me, Faye.
I want you to have the gifts
from Odessa, the amber beads
lost in a crack in the sidewalk,
the afghan Ima crocheted,
the Coptic silk on the wall —
threads of saffron, vermillion,
aquamarine.

Come with me, Faye.
We'll untangle roots beneath streetlamps,
wind through the maze
of apricot churches
and blue minarets.
I came here to find the house
they burned in the pogrom,
Podgorny Street where ancient
kilims twist down from sills
and gloom falls like dust.

I never told you how my father
read to us from the Torah
by candlelight in the cellar,
how I fled alone in a hurry,
leaving our story behind.
I must find the jewels
left in the rocks.
Come with me!

LENA

Return: Podgorny Street

The sign over the window:
M. Russak and Sons, We Make Suits.
From somewhere a woman's voice —
Kiss the mezzuzah before you enter.
I touch the tiny scroll
and cross the threshold.

The tailor shop in the front room,
Tateh stooped over the Singer,
his sidelocks wispy and pale.
When I reach through
the frayed light,
he fades.

The clock ticks in the kitchen,
the kettle hisses. Ima sits
at the porcelain table
humming as she peels potatoes.
She turns toward me,
hovers, then disappears.

I push back the curtain:
in the courtyard, sheets
and shirts looped on the line,
Ima hunched against crumbling stone.
Tateh calls her inside.

Down the hall in their bedroom
they lie in the twine of sleep.
Should I wake them? Should I leave?
Loose threads unravel in the dark.

SILK WEAVINGS

LENA

At Pearl's Convalescent Home

Dear Morris,

Slowly I come back to life
through a different door.

Mornings I take the path through the woods,
nights I watch herons wade in the lake.

Pearl brews Russian *chai,*
a *chinik* steams on the table.

From the window, white torsos of trees,
a blue field of light.

Don't dream too much, you once said.
But until I dream, nothing's real.

Sometimes I still dream Odessa,
the boardwalk and the hundred steps to the sea,

sometimes the night they sailed into the fire.
Wait for us to return, they said.

Again and again I've gone back to find them.
But I'm not dreaming now.

Here we gather apples from bent trees.
Come soon.

I'll show you the lake
and the long winding trail.

Love, Lena

FAYE

Sunday Rally, Union Square

Across the Hudson on the Weehawken ferry,
Papa, Ben, Ezra and me. On Broadway,
trolleys rumble over the tracks,
sparks fly, even streetlamps wobble!

When we reach Union Square,
girls Papa knows from the mill —
Lottie Smith, Mamie Carroll —
are handing out leaflets. Boys
hoist banners. A man stands
on a box and shouts,

Strikers in North Carolina
sprayed with bullets.
Mother of four dead on the picket line.
We want justice now!

Crowds mill about. Policemen on horseback
gallop by flashing guns. *Don't be afraid,*
Papa says, *as long as we're peaceful,*
they'll leave us alone.
He buys us knishes.

Arm in arm with the marchers,
we stream out of the park, past
bookstalls, pushcarts, haberdasheries
and used clothing stores,
singing all the way from 14th to 5th...

We will build a new world
We will build a new world some day...aa...ay...

Oh, oh, deep in my heart I do believe
we will build a new world some day.

This is America, Papa says,
and it's better than a picture show!

FAYE

Night Bird

Alone in the kitchen, I chop carrots,
parsnips, leeks, put a chicken
in a pot and turn on Papa's Philco.

The red light glows, the piano rolls,
a gravelly voice croons,
I can't give you anything but love, ba bee...

The trumpet blares, I sway to the beat,
How's my flock out there, my nightbirds?
I hope you're dancing!

I see him in a ballroom
high over the Hudson in top hat
and tails and he's singing to me,

Gee I'd like to see you looking swell, ba bee...
The saxophone moans, I stir the soup,
add parsley and dill,

kick off my shoes and shimmy
into the parlor, a girl alone in the dark,
a night bird, barefoot and dancing.

LENA

At Fairview I Lived in a Wild Grove

Beyond the bars, I saw menorahs
lit in the trees, the tip of each branch
a candle flame.

Singed birds fell to earth,
blood trickled down walls.
Night after night, the charred stench

of flesh, the metallic taste of death.
I crouched in a corner,
pulled a robe over my eyes.

They fed me pills, strapped me
to the bed. I heard thorny cries —
were they mine?

An orchard of fruit and seeds
flew in and out. I shook the boughs.
Fiery apples fell into my lap.

At Fairview I lived in a wild grove.
At Fairview I had no roof
over my head.

FAYE

Rugelah, 5 A.M.

The house is dark and breathing
deep under the covers.
I tiptoe to the kitchen,
lift bowls from the shelf,
mix cream cheese and butter.
Flour dusts my fingers
as I roll dough into a circle,
spread blackberry jam
with the back of a spoon
the way Mama taught me.
I work quickly, leaning over,
sprinkling nuts and raisins
on top, my hands
shaping ovals, folding,
crimping edges.

Light sifts through the windows
and I think of Mama, coming
home after so many months,
how we baked before dawn,
I, barefoot, she in nightgown
and slippers. Now I slide
the tray into the oven
and glide through the quiet
to wait for the rising.

FAYE

She's Coming Home

I lay two yards of oilcloth
on the table to hide the nick
Ezra made, smooth the folds,
scallop the edges, set sprigs

of parsley in a jar. Next, I
soak dingy curtains in suds,
shine windows til they gleam,
polish the samovar Mama loves.

Now the room's washed in light —
It splashes chairs, flecks
the linoleum, makes tassels
of light on the walls.

I bleach towels white,
iron sheets, line shelves.
Every plate, every knife,
every spoon is in place.

Ezra says I hold things down.
He calls me a stone.
I don't mind.
I like to set things right.

FAYE

I'm Not the Girl I Used to Be

Where are the curtains? she asks.
And why did you cover my table?
I don't say a word.
She pulls off the new oilcloth.
I'm like a stone.

I'm not the girl I used to be.
Now when she wakes me at 3 A.M.,
Fayela, bring me toast and tea.
I say no, it's late, go back to sleep.

Sad Mama. Loose in her bed.
Already hiding, already
rummaging inside the past.
Every hour I listen for her anxious breath.
Will this ever end?

Will she roam the nights again
wearing the handkerchief turban?
Will I find her out on the curb
talking to strangers
or alone on the fire escape
flapping her arms like a bird?

FAYE

I Keep My Secrets Now

Papa gave me a diary with a lock and key.
So late at night I keep my secrets…

> Today on the street two boys yelled at me,
> *Hey, Jew girl, furriner,*
> *you and your crazy Mama.*
> I don't say a word. I'm a stone.
> I keep walking.

> In America you *can* walk away
> but not in Odessa. There was nowhere to go.
> Pogroms, pogroms everywhere.

> Sometimes I dream backward.
> I see Mama, a girl in a closet,
> hiding. She waits for hours,
> then opens the door, steps
> past burning bodies.

> *Leave, Mama,* I cry, *or the Cossacks*
> *will come back to find you.*
> Mama's not crazy but she can't leave Odessa.
> Again and again she sees
> her whole family trapped in flames.

> Mama's not crazy.
> She's like the cracked bowl Papa fixed.
> If I could, I would mend her.

MORRIS

The Watchman

Sunday at five A.M., I startle awake.
A rustling chorus under the eaves,
the whir of wings. Lena's already up
sipping tea from her favorite cup,
the gold-rimmed one I've kept safe
high on a shelf away from the boys.

Now I see the girl I found in Pabianice,
the orphan girl dressed in rags,
her face, her wistful gaze,
the girl who danced for me
one summer night.

When we met I tried to wake her
from old nightmares but
her heart was already ruptured.
I held her when we lowered
Daniel's casket into the sea,
when we buried Rachel,
when she wailed for hours
in the dark.

Then, for years I could not think
what to do. I watched from a distance.
I could not endure her wild flights.
Now I'll sit close, a watchman
at the kitchen table,
a husband shelling peas
while she stews apricots.

MORRIS

The Bath

I'd love one, she says,
and I draw the bath,
unbutton her blouse,
lay the tumble of clothes
on the bed and lift her up...

I thought I might never
hold her like this again,
her whole weight
in my arms, her fingers
wrapped around mine
as she sinks into the tub,
her nipples dark
in the silvery blue.

I set a towel on the ledge,
Morris, I'm sorry...she says,
Sha, I say, kneeling beside her,
squeezing the sponge,
spilling water down
the curve of her neck.

I feel her calm
as she leans back.
She's not dreaming now —
hair wet and curled
in the steamy heat,
arms raised over her head.

FAYE

At Brothers Department Store, Downtown

Aisles of cloches, lavender stockings,
ropes of crystal and pearl.
Our heels click on pink marble floors.
Wherever we turn, something new —
bakelite bracelets, marcasite rings,
rouge even for knees.
We dab our wrists:
Shalimar, Evening in Paris!

We could lose ourselves here, Mama says,
wrapping herself in a feather boa.
Is this too much? Do you want to rest?
I've had a long time to rest.
She takes my hand.
But we can have tea.

The Tulip Garden on the mezzanine —
deep leather banquettes, porcelain cups.
A few months ago she lay limp
on the bed, face to the wall.
Now she steps lightly onto the lift.
An usher in white suit
and gloves escorts us up.
Lingerie, Ladies' Apparel on 3!

Peach satin slips, lace pajamas,
a fringed sheath scooped low in the back.
This year prints are the rage,
the saleslady says.
Mama drapes a paisley shawl over her shoulders.
I try on a yellow silk dress.
We stare at ourselves in the beveled mirror.
You look beautiful, Mama.
You are beautiful, Faye.

I Tell My Children About the Scalping in 1912

This is the story of Camella Viol.
She came to work at Hamil's Mill
when she was ten. "Your daughter's
tall," the boss told her father, "give
me four dollars and we'll make her
fourteen."

We heard the scream, saw the machine
suck in Camella's hair, tearing the flesh
from her scalp. Blood spurted over the
silk, leaked onto the floor. I lifted her
onto a stretcher, watched as they
wheeled her away.

This is the story of Camella Viol,
who lay for weeks in a hospital room,
bandages wrapped round the wound.
When I went to see her she cried,
I have a gash that won't go away.
Will my hair ever come back?

I heard that the boss came to see her
and warned, "Don't say a word or
someone you love will be hurt."
Now she wears a cap to hide
the place where hair never grows.
And at Hamil's Mill the machines
knock back and forth night and day
but Camella Viol keeps still.

LENA

The Balance

The sky from my window
is sapphire and ash
the last light of day

Everything's quiet
even the birds
are not disturbed

Mrs. Greevey's cat
a queen at the sill
lies half asleep

On the street
rooms glow like tents
in the cool October air

This is the time
I like best — the mind
loosens its tangled threads

the body curls into itself
tipping the scales
toward night

The Matreshka Dolls on the Dresser

Hidden inside me
is a doll.
She looks exactly
like me
but she's smaller.
And hidden
inside her
is another.
Her cheeks
like mine
are ripe plums
and she too
wears a babushka.
We all fit
inside each other,
we're all
pear-shaped
little mothers.
At the center
we open,
except the last one,
the tiny one.
She's a seed
waiting.

FAYE

Wedding Gown

I've learned plackets and pleats,
practiced on scraps of slippery satin.
I can face collars, turn cuffs.
Mr. Cohen asks me to sew
the gown for the millowner's
daughter. I lay the rustling
folds over my shoulders,
rub the papery skin
against my cheek:

Antique crepe de chine!

Someday I'll sew my own wedding gown.
It will be simple — no bows,
no hoops, no swags of cloth
draped from the waist —
just Alençon lace
set in the vee of the neckline,
silk-covered buttons
straight down the back.

FAYE

Silkworm Dream

In my dream a silkworm spins
a thousand strands around herself,
then lies inside a dark cocoon.

Does she like the binding
weight and cover? Is she
content to dream of light?

Her eyes are closed,
her oozing body stilled.
But coiled for days and nights

behind those silent walls,
she starts to twist and turn,
unwinding from the tangled skein

of sleep. Her shell begins to crack,
her crumpled wings unfold
and up she climbs the fragile thread.

FAYE/LENA

Silk Rhapsody

i. Faye

Mama, you never told me
they hid you in a closet
before the Cossacks
set them on fire.
You never told me
you found
their scorched bones,
then walked alone
across mountains,
a girl my age,
barefoot on stone.

ii. Lena

Yes, Faye, their souls flew up
around me, their wings fluttered
along the dark road.
I walked through December,
wandered through smoke
until I found Pabianice.

For years I hoarded my madness,
I liked my wild grove —
then Fairview — all those swarming bees,
those strangers crowding,
all speaking at once.
I was nervous, scared
to turn, scared not to turn.
At Fairview, the sun
followed me everywhere —
it had no back.

iii. Faye

Mama, we lived so long
in a house on fire.
We were all caught in your flames.
I felt the scorch on my face.
But now you send me to the river.
Go be a girl, you say.

iv. Lena

Wake slowly, Faye.
Be like the rose.
Let leafy trees sway as you pass.
Glide like silk over stones.
Dip into the stream.
You can enter the light.

v. Faye

The river waits.
I climb down the fire escape
out onto the path.
I take no coat
no purse, no key.
Only the moon watches.

Here   now   in this moment
fire and water are mine.
I stroke the air.
My arms are wheels
turning up and back.
It is morning   it is night.
The gate is open.

THE LANGUAGE OF SILK

Dyeing Silk

The women are dyeing indigo
heads wrapped in turbans

they bend to bowls
of crushed leaves

pour water over ash
from sun up to sundown

they soak cloth
dye stains their fingers

even their lips have a bluish cast
their arms turn blue

when they lift the silk
from the cool bath

lift and wring   lift and wring
the women are singing

they have learned to unravel light
all afternoon

shimmering silk
dries in the sun

the women stand
in bare feet

folding cloth into bundles
tying threads

their hips ache
as dusk fades into night

they stitch robes
mend ragged seams

cradle their young
in indigo shawls

everything rinsed
with the print of their hands

dipped in the blue bowl
of their secrets

everything found
in the language of silk

GLOSSARY

alta kop	old head
astrakhan	baby lamb fur
babushka	kerchief
berioska	department store in Russian
challah	braided loaf of glazed egg bread
chinik	tea pot
daven	pray
Forward	Yiddish newspaper
golem	in Jewish folklore, a magical figure created of clay in the form of a man and endowed with life
Hasidim	sect of Jewish mystics that originated in Poland during the eighteenth century, emphasizing joyful worship
hazzan	cantor, a trained professional singer of religious liturgy
Ima	mother in Hebrew
Kabbala	Jewish mysticism, tradition of esoteric thought
Kaddish	Jewish prayer of mourning, which affirms life and hope
Khazars	ancient Turkic people believed by some to have been the ancestors of many East European Jews. The eighth-century Khazar nobility embraced Judaism.
klezmer	informal itinerant music of the shtetl
kneidlach	matzo balls, used in chicken soup
Lodz	city in Poland, silk weaving center
luftmensch	a dreamy sensitive person, one with his or her head in the clouds

mandelbrot	sweet almond bread
matreshka	family of dolls of Russian origin, also called nesting dolls and mother dolls
menorah	a candelabrum with many branches
meshuga	crazy
mezzuzah	doorpost affixed to front door jamb, consecrating the home
Pabianice	town in Poland, near city of Lodz where Lena lived after leaving Russia
rebbe	a learned man
rugelah	a little cake
schena meidela	Yiddish, good little girl
sheitel	Yiddish, wig traditionally worn by orthodox Jewish Ashkenazi women in Eastern Europe after they married
shtetl	village in East European countries where Jews could live and their culture flourish
shul	synagogue
tallis	prayer shawl used by males at religious services
Tateh	father in Yiddish
Torah	the Five Books of Moses
Workmen's Circle	Jewish men's social club
yarmulke	skullcap worn by males at services
zaddik	spiritual leader of the Hasidic community
Zohar	the Book of Splendor and other metaphysical texts on Kabbala that appeared in Spain in the thirteenth century

ACKNOWLEDGMENTS

Some of these poems, in slightly different versions, appeared originally in the following publications:

Calyx: "Dyeing Silk"
Creative Showcase, Fashion Institute of Technology:
"The Kosmos"
Paterson Literary Review: "Blue Silk"
Rising, South Mountain Anthology: "Lost Amber"
U.S.1 Worksheets: "M. Russak and Sons, We Make Suits"
Voices International: "On the Black Sea in Odessa"

"Berliner Coats" is based in part on a story
depicting factory conditions in Emma Goldman's
Living My Life.

"I Tell My Children about the Scalping in 1912" is adapted
from an incident that took place in a mill in Lawrence,
Massachusetts.

Lines have been excerpted from the following songs:
"I Can't Give You Anything but Love" (lyrics by
Dorothy Fields)
"Tumbalalaika" (old Jewish folksong)
"Solidarity Forever" (adapted by Ralph Chapin from the
"Battle Hymn of the Republic")
"We Shall Overcome" (gospel song)

I am grateful to the New Jersey State Council on the Arts, the Corporation of Yaddo, the Dodge Foundation, and the Virginia Center for the Creative Arts for grants that enabled me to work on this book.

Thanks to Carol Goodman, Amy Gash, Barbara Morcheles, Mary Christensen, Dorothy Ryan, Beth Bahler, and especially to Ann Wallace and Susan Jackson for their sustained insight in helping to shape these poems. Michelle Cameron offered computer skills and literary judgement precisely when I needed them. My heart-felt thanks to Joan Cusack Handler for her generosity, encouragement, and vision. And to Molly Peacock, who has shared her good sense and poetic wisdom, I owe gratitude and much more.